Ukulele Picking Tunes

EARLY MUSIC GEMS

Ondřej Šárek

Acacia Solid Concert Ukulele ACS-C cover image courtesy of Lanikai Ukuleles.

WWW.MELBAY.COM

Preface

This book presents 34 wonderful Early Music melodies arranged for ukulele solo in standard gCEA tuning. The tunes range from the early Renaissance to the Baroque era. All of the solos are arranged in notation and tablature. The slur markings are subjective and I encourage you to add stylistic effects such as slides, hammer-ons, pull-offs and more as you interpret the melodies. It is my practice to use the "campanella" style; in order to play in this manner you will need to keep your left-hand fingers on the ukulele fingerboard as long as possible to let the strings continue to ring. These melodies are fun to play and timeless in their beauty and vitality. I hope you enjoy playing them.

Ondřej Šárek

Index of Tunes

Adoro Devote

13th Century Plainsong

Moderately Slow ♩ = 64

Allegro

Anonymous

Alman

Robert Johnson

Rhythmically ♩ = 112

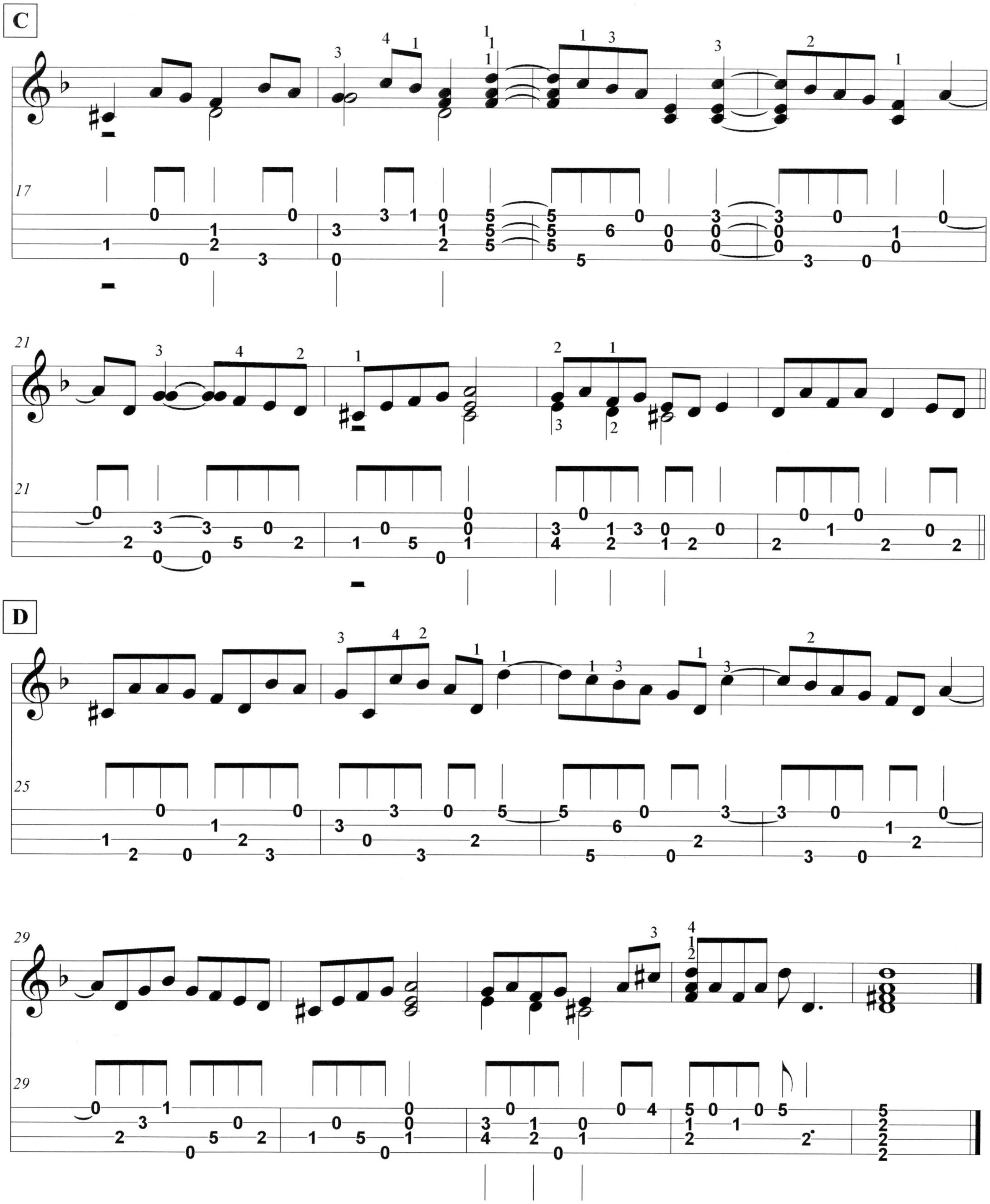
C
17
21
D
25
29

An Italian Rant

John Playford

Andante

Anonymous

Ballade

Anonymous

Bear Dance

Branle Double

Michael Praetorius

D
E

Canarios

Gasper Sanz

Chestnut

John Playford

Childgrove

Rhythmically 𝅗𝅥 = 74

Playford Collection

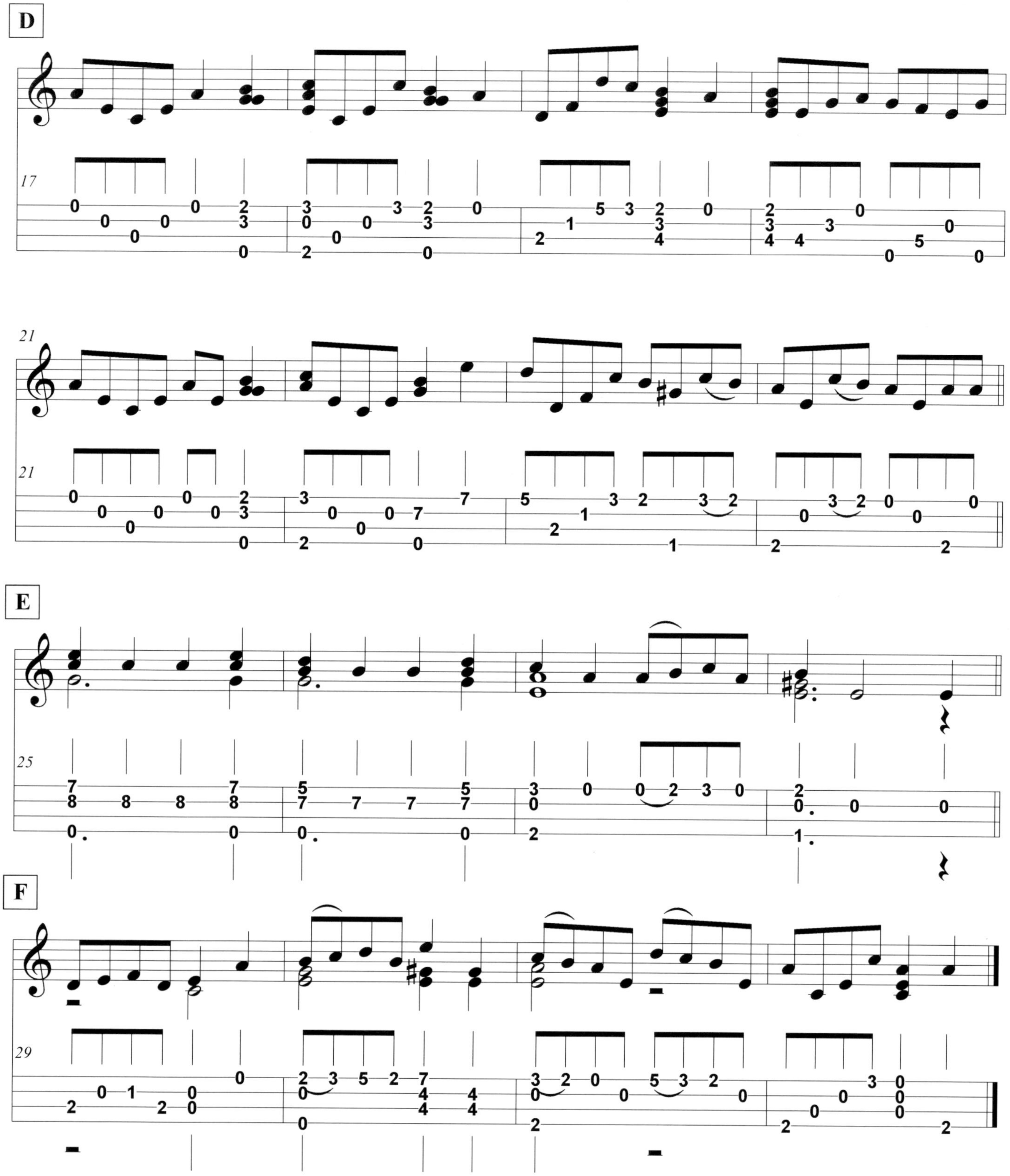
D
17
21
21
E
25
F
29

Come With Me, My Giselle

Adam de la Halle

Andante ♩ = 74

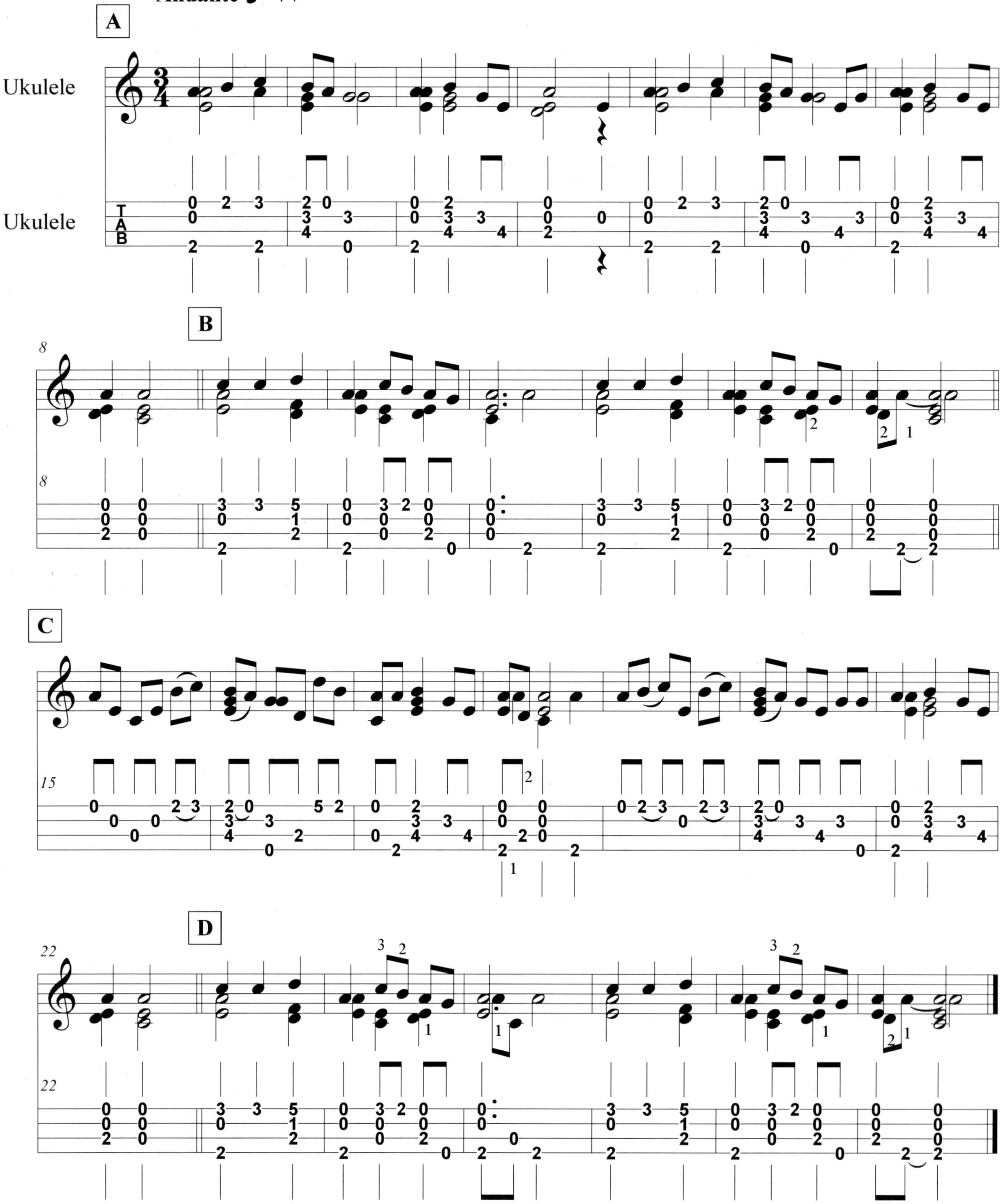

This page has been left blank to avoid an awkward page turn.

Dont vient cela

Susato

Danserye 1551

Fortune My Foe

B

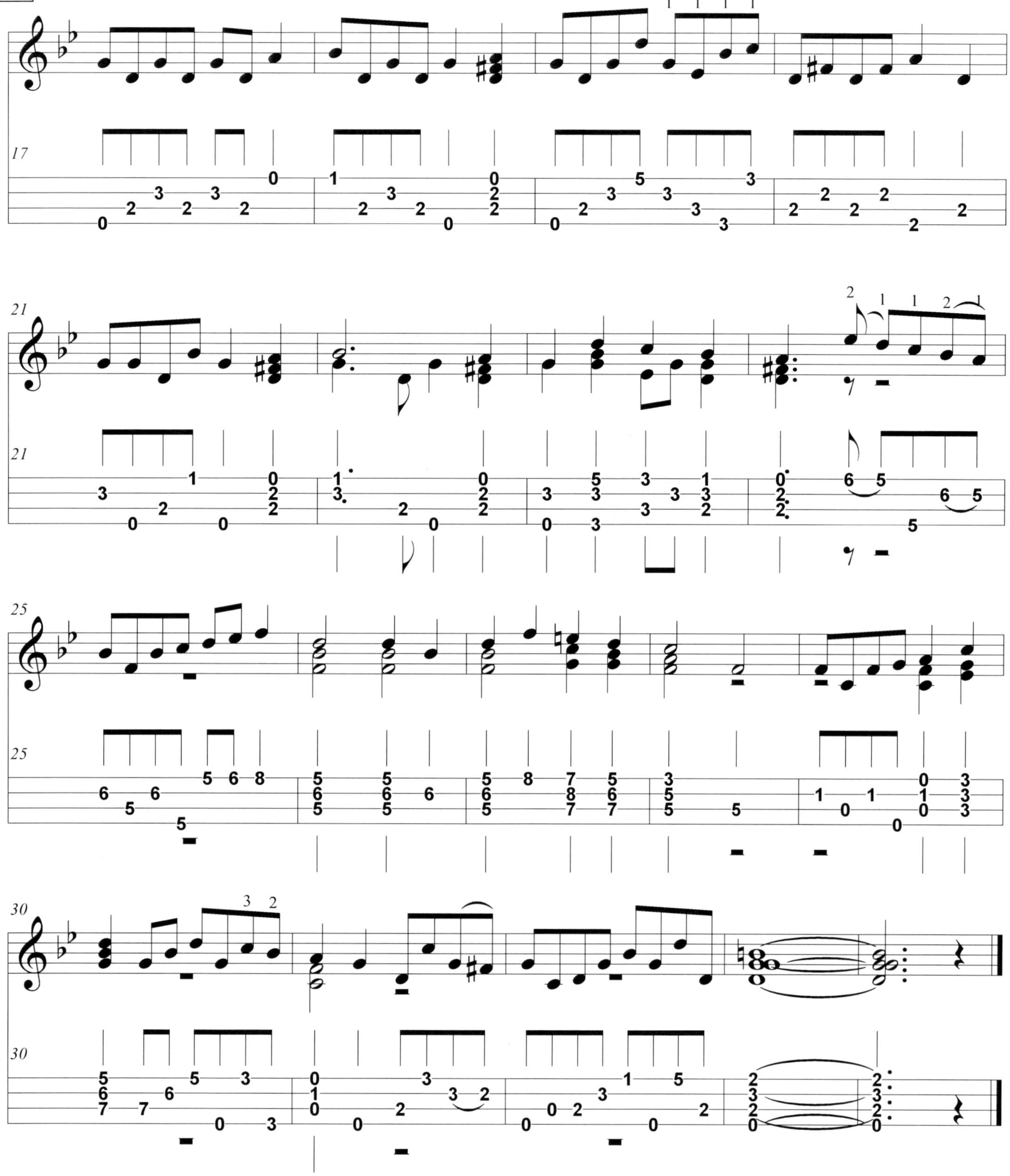

Gavotte

Michael Praetorius

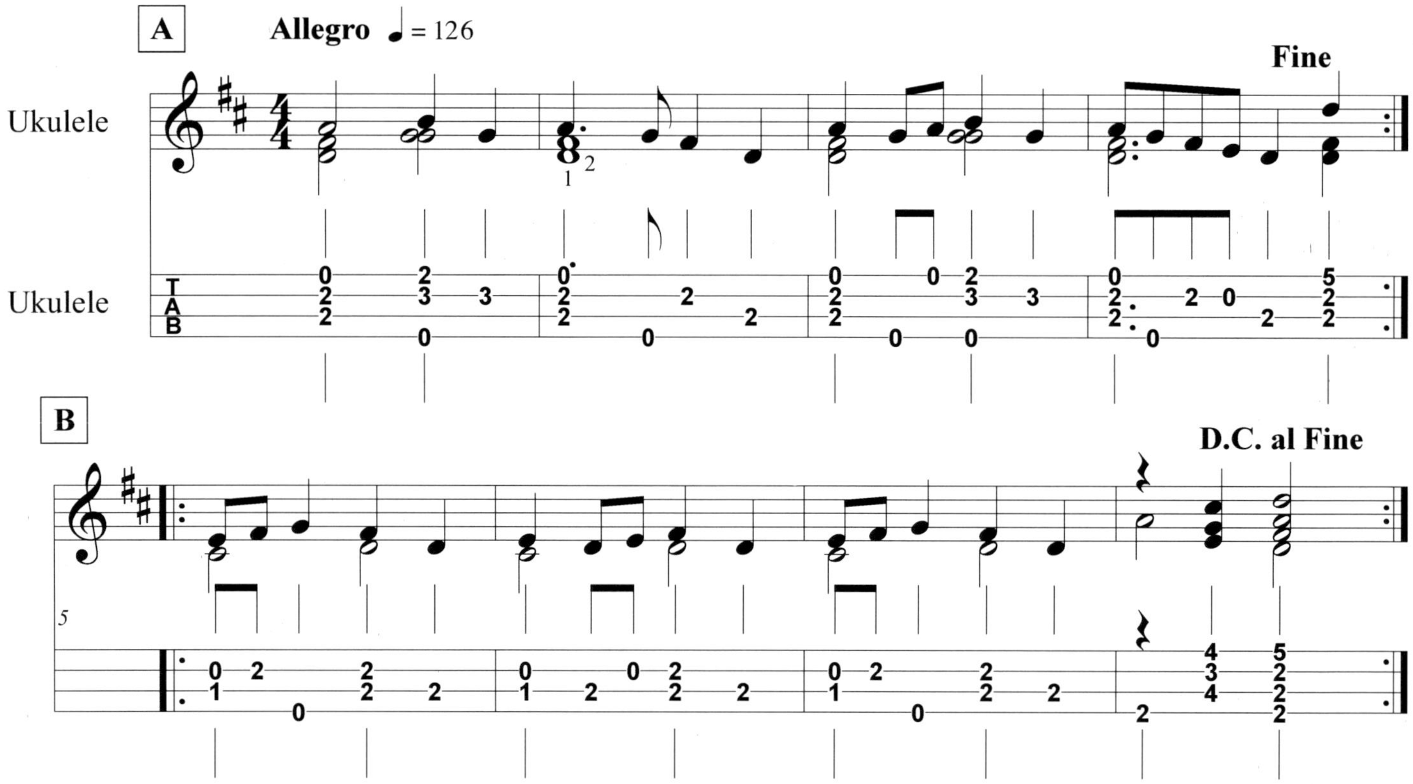

Greensleeves

C
D

E

Grimstock

C

D

Guardeme las vacas

Luis de Narvaez

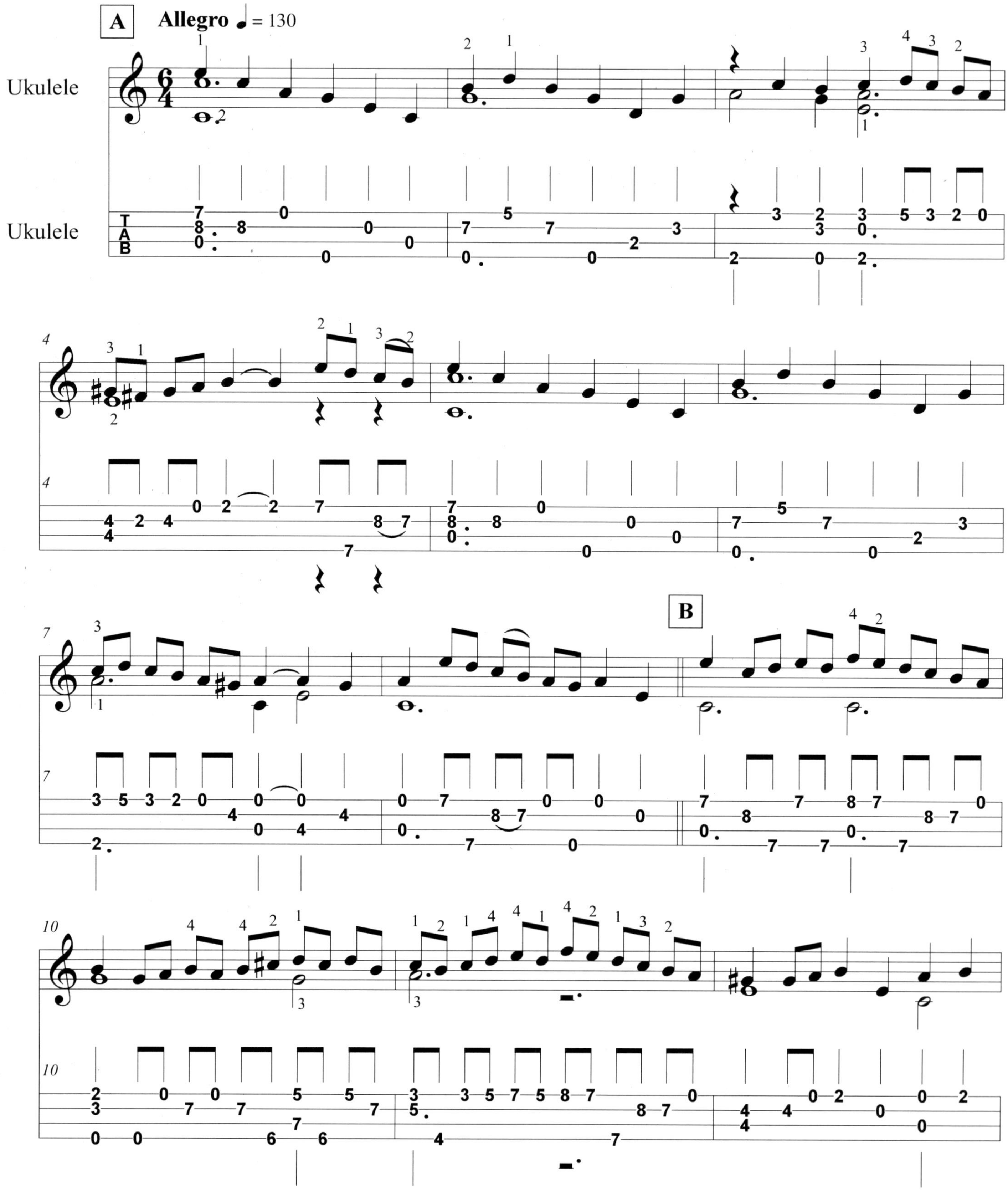

C

D

This page has been left blank to avoid an awkward page turn.

Kemp's Jig

21
D
26
31
E
36

La Folias

Gaspar Sanz

C

Moderato

Anonymous

C
D

O Esca Viatorum

Louis Bourgeois 1549

Packington's Pound

C

Pastourelle

13th Century French

D
27
34
E
41
48

Rendez à Dieu

Louis Bourgeois 1543

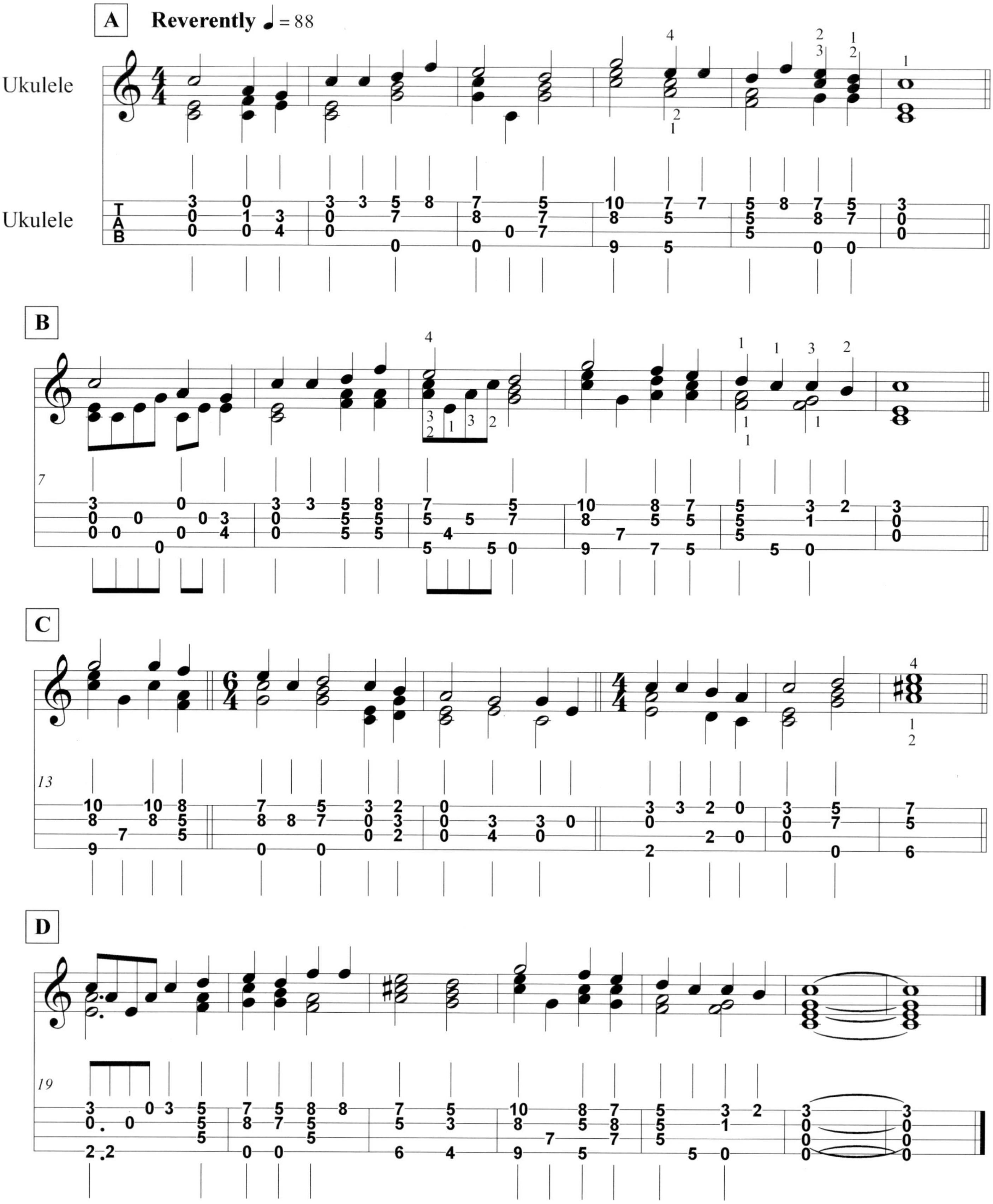

St. Martin's

Moderato ♩ = 126

John Playford

Saltarello

Vincenzo Galilei

D
E
F

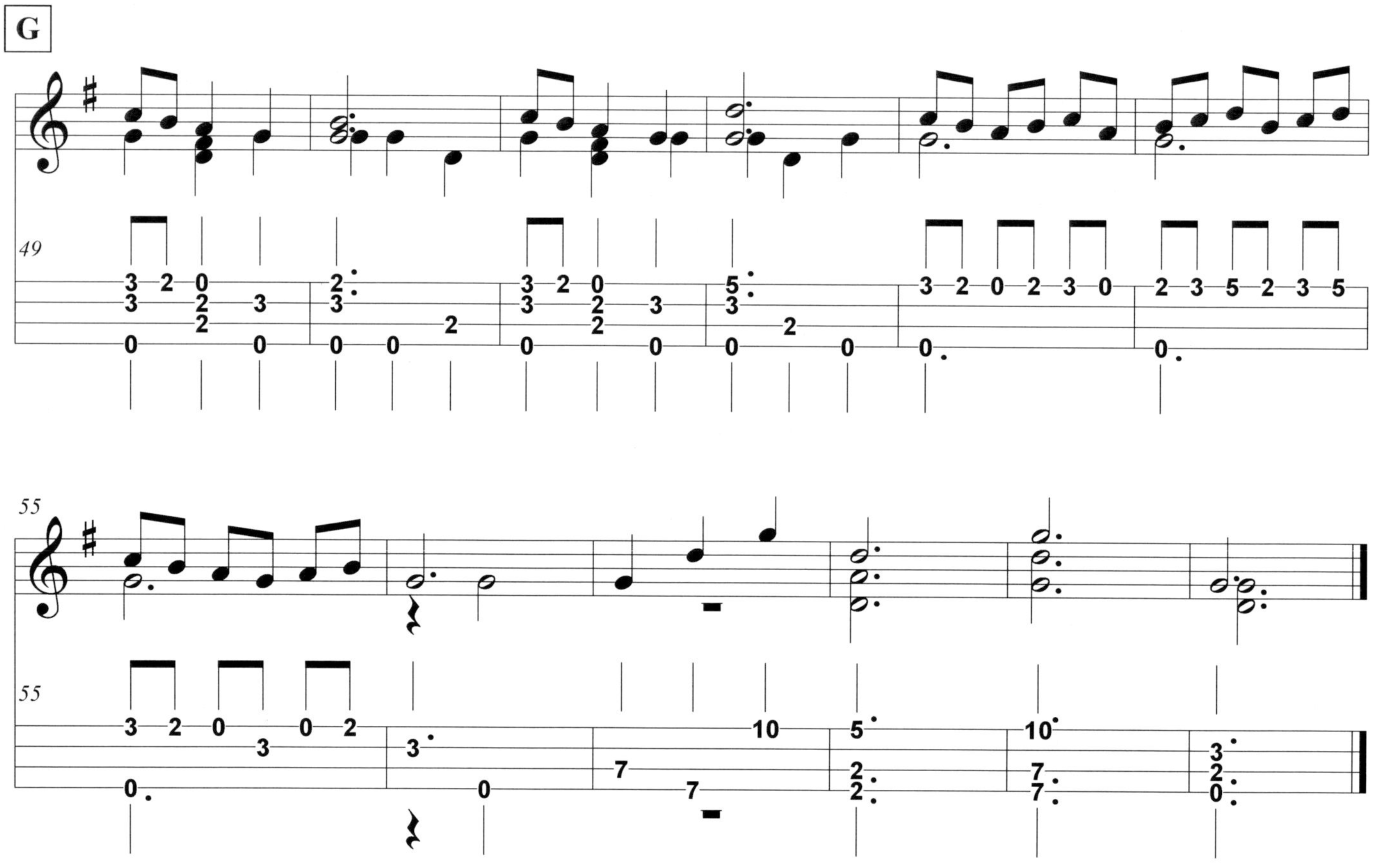
G
49
55

Si Pour

C
D

Spagnoletta

Moderato ♩ = 144

Michael Praetorious

To Drive the Cold Winter Away

Tutte Venite Armati

Volte

Michael Praetorius

Wilson's Wilde

On the Cold Ground

John Playford

Moderato ♩. = 74

Other Recommended Mel Bay Ukulele Books

20 Caribbean Pieces for Ukulele (Carr)
20 Celtic Fingerstyle Uke Tunes (MacKillop)
20 Easy Classical Uke Pieces for Kids (MacKillop)
20 Old-Time American Tunes Arranged for Ukulele (MacKillop)
20 Popular Uke Tunes for Kids (MacKillop)
20 Spanish Baroque Pieces by Gaspar Sanz Arranged for Uke (MacKillop)
Children's Songs for Solo Ukulele (Carr)
Classics for Ukulele (Šárek)
Famous Solos and Duets for the Ukulele (King)
Favorite Classical Themes for Ukulele (Coe)
Favorite Fingerstyle Solos for Ukulele (Nelson)
Favorite Old-Time American Songs for Ukulele (Nelson)
Fingerstyle Duets for Ukulele (Nelson)
First Jams: Ukulele (Andrews)
Folk Songs for Solo Ukulele (Carr)
Francisco Tárrega for Ukulele (Šárek)
Gospel Favorites for Solo Ukulele (Carr)
Great Melodies for Solo Ukulele (Carr)
Hawaiian Uke Tunebook (Eidson/Cherednik)
Holiday Favorites for Solo Ukulele (Carr)
Indie Rock Uke (Driscoll)
Leopold Mozart's Notebook for Wolfgang Arranged for Ukulele (Šarek)
Mauro Giuliani Arranged for Ukulele Duet (Šárek)
Sacred Music for Ukulele (Dempler)
Songs & Solos for Uke (Eidson/Cherednik)
The Bach Uke Book (MacKillop)
Ukulele Bluegrass Solos (Šárek)
Ukulele Chord Solos in C Tuning (N. Griffn)
Ukulele Christmas Carols (Andrews)
Ukulele Duets (Carr)
50 Three-Chord Christmas Songs for Guitar, Banjo and Uke (McCabe)
Favorite Old-Time American Songs for Ukulele (Nelson)
Favorite Uke Tunes (N. Jones)
Fun with Folk Songs (M. Bay)
Sacred Music for Ukulele (Dempler)
Sing and Strum: 7 Hawaiian Favorites for Ukulele (Kimura)
Songs & Solos for Uke (Eidson/Cherednik)
Ten Favorite Hawaiian Songs (Kimura)
The Cat's Meow: Songs from the Roaring 20's (Whitcomb)
Uke Ballads: A Treasury of 25 Love Songs Old and New (Whitcomb)
Uke Tunes Made Easy (W. Bay)
Ukulele Christmas Carols (Andrews)
Ukulele Heaven: Songs from the Golden Age of the Ukulele (Whitcomb)
Ukulele Jamboree! (Whitcomb)
Ukulele Party (Moore)